my FAVORITE RECIPES

A create-your-own cookbook!

Gooseberry Patch
2500 Farmers Dr., #110
Columbus, OH 43235

www.gooseberrypatch.com
1·800·854·6673

Copyright 2006, Gooseberry Patch 978-1-933494-11-1
Second Printing, January, 2011

Do you have a tried & true recipe...
tip, craft or memory that you'd like to see featured in a **Gooseberry
Patch** book? Visit our website at **www.gooseberrypatch.com**, register
and follow the easy steps to submit your favorite family recipe.
Or send them to us at:

Gooseberry Patch
Attn: Book Dept.
2500 Farmers Dr., #110
Delaware, OH 43015

Don't forget to include the number of servings your recipe makes,
plus your name, street address, phone number and e-mail address.
If we select your recipe, your name will appear right along with
it...and you'll receive a **FREE** copy of the book!

Contents

Recipe Name: Chocolate Chip Pie   **Serves:** 8

Ingredients:

1/2 c. all purpose flour

1/2 c. sugar

1/2 c. brown sugar, packed

2 eggs, beaten

3/4 c. butter, softened

1 c. semi-sweet chocolate chips

1 c. chopped walnuts

9-inch pie crust, unbaked

Directions:

Blend flour, sugar and brown sugar into eggs; add butter, mixing well. Fold in chocolate chips and walnuts; pour into pie crust. Bake at 325° for 55 to 60 minutes or until knife inserted into the middle of the pie comes out clean.

My Favorite
Breakfast
RECIPES

NOTES

_____
_____
_____
_____
_____
_____
_____
_____
_____
_____

Recipe Name: _____ **Serves:** _____

Ingredients:

_____   _____

_____   _____

_____   _____

_____   _____

_____   _____

_____   _____

Directions:

_____

_____

_____

_____

_____

_____

_____

_____

_____

_____

_____

_____

_____

_____

_____

_____

Recipe Name: _____ **Serves:** _____

Ingredients:

_____   _____
_____   _____
_____   _____
_____   _____
_____   _____
_____   _____

Directions:

_____
_____
_____
_____
_____
_____
_____
_____
_____
_____
_____
_____
_____
_____
_____

Sweet cider-glazed sausages
are a treat at breakfast. Brown
1/2 pound breakfast sausages
in a skillet and drain. Add a
cup of apple cider and simmer
for about 10 minutes.

Recipe Name: _____ **Serves:** _____

Ingredients:

_____   _____
_____   _____
_____   _____
_____   _____
_____   _____
_____   _____
_____   _____

Directions:

_____
_____
_____
_____
_____
_____
_____
_____
_____
_____
_____
_____
_____
_____
_____
_____
_____
_____
_____

Recipe Name: _____ **Serves:** _____

Ingredients:

_____   _____

_____   _____

_____   _____

_____   _____

_____   _____

_____   _____

_____   _____

Directions:

_____

_____

_____

_____

_____

_____

_____

_____

_____

_____

_____

_____

_____

_____

_____

_____

_____

_____

Recipe Name: _____   **Serves:** _____

Ingredients:

_____   _____
_____   _____
_____   _____
_____   _____
_____   _____
_____   _____
_____   _____

Directions:

_____
_____
_____
_____
_____
_____
_____
_____
_____
_____
_____
_____
_____
_____
_____

Make raspberry butter quickly by combining one cup butter, 2 cups powdered sugar and 10 ounces frozen raspberries, thawed. Mix until smooth...delicious!

Recipe Name: _____ **Serves:** _____

Ingredients:

_____   _____

_____   _____

_____   _____

_____   _____

_____   _____

_____   _____

Directions:

_____

_____

_____

_____

_____

_____

_____

_____

_____

_____

_____

_____

_____

_____

_____

_____

_____

Recipe Name: _____   **Serves:** _____

Ingredients:

_____   _____

_____   _____

_____   _____

_____   _____

_____   _____

_____   _____

_____

Directions:

_____

_____

_____

_____

_____

_____

_____

_____

_____

_____

_____

_____

_____

_____

_____

_____

_____

_____

Recipe Name: _____   **Serves:** _____

Ingredients:

_____   _____

_____   _____

_____   _____

_____   _____

_____   _____

_____   _____

_____   _____

Directions:

_____

_____

_____

_____

_____

_____

_____

_____

_____

_____

_____

_____

_____

_____

_____

_____

_____

_____

Recipe Name: _____   **Serves:** _____

Ingredients:

_____   _____
_____   _____
_____   _____
_____   _____
_____   _____
_____   _____
_____   _____

Directions:

_____
_____
_____
_____
_____
_____
_____
_____
_____
_____
_____
_____
_____
_____
_____
_____
_____
_____
_____

Recipe Name: _____   **Serves:** _____

Ingredients:

_____   _____
_____   _____
_____   _____
_____   _____
_____   _____
_____   _____

Directions:

_____
_____
_____
_____
_____
_____
_____
_____
_____
_____
_____
_____
_____
_____

A bowl filled with bright lemons and limes looks so cheery on a breakfast table...prick them a few times with a fork to release their delightful scent.

Recipe Name: _____ **Serves:** _____

Ingredients:

_____   _____

_____   _____

_____   _____

_____   _____

_____   _____

_____   _____

Directions:

_____

_____

_____

_____

_____

_____

_____

_____

_____

_____

_____

_____

_____

_____

_____

_____

_____

_____

_____

Recipe Name: _____ **Serves:** _____

Ingredients:

_____   _____
_____   _____
_____   _____
_____   _____
_____   _____
_____   _____
_____

Directions:

_____
_____
_____
_____
_____
_____
_____
_____
_____
_____
_____
_____
_____
_____
_____
_____
_____
_____

Recipe Name: _____   **Serves:** _____

Ingredients:

_____   _____

_____   _____

_____   _____

_____   _____

_____   _____

_____   _____

Directions:

_____

_____

_____

_____

_____

_____

_____

_____

_____

_____

_____

_____

_____

_____

_____

Vintage-style salt shakers quickly become the prettiest little containers for dusting powdered sugar or cinnamon on breakfast treats.

Recipe Name: _____ **Serves:** _____

Ingredients:

_____   _____

_____   _____

_____   _____

_____   _____

_____   _____

_____   _____

_____   _____

Directions:

_____

_____

_____

_____

_____

_____

_____

_____

_____

_____

_____

_____

_____

_____

_____

_____

_____

_____

Breakfasts

Recipe Name: _____ **Serves:** _____

Ingredients:

_____   _____
_____   _____
_____   _____
_____   _____
_____   _____
_____   _____
_____

Directions:

_____
_____
_____
_____
_____
_____
_____
_____
_____
_____
_____
_____
_____
_____
_____
_____
_____
_____

Recipe Name: _____ **Serves:** _____

Ingredients:

_____   _____
_____   _____
_____   _____
_____   _____
_____   _____
_____   _____

Directions:

_____
_____
_____
_____
_____
_____
_____
_____
_____
_____
_____
_____
_____
_____
_____
_____
_____
_____

Recipe Name: _____ **Serves:** _____

Ingredients:

_____   _____

_____   _____

_____   _____

_____   _____

_____   _____

_____   _____

Directions:

_____

_____

_____

_____

_____

_____

_____

_____

_____

_____

_____

_____

_____

_____

_____

_____

_____

_____

Recipe Name: _____ **Serves:** _____

Ingredients:

_____   _____

_____   _____

_____   _____

_____   _____

_____   _____

_____   _____

Directions:

_____

_____

_____

_____

_____

_____

_____

_____

_____

_____

_____

_____

_____

_____

Serve your fluffy hotcakes or waffles
with flair...instead of setting a plastic
bottle on the table, serve warm syrup
in small cream pitchers or
a vintage syrup server.

Recipe Name: _____ **Serves:** _____

Ingredients:

_____   _____

_____   _____

_____   _____

_____   _____

_____   _____

_____   _____

_____   _____

Directions:

_____

_____

_____

_____

_____

_____

_____

_____

_____

_____

_____

_____

_____

_____

_____

_____

_____

_____

_____

My Favorite
Appetizer
RECIPES

NOTES

_____

_____

_____

_____

_____

_____

_____

_____

_____

Recipe Name: _____ **Serves:** _____

Ingredients:

_____   _____
_____   _____
_____   _____
_____   _____
_____   _____
_____   _____
_____

Directions:

_____
_____
_____
_____
_____
_____
_____
_____
_____
_____
_____
_____
_____
_____
_____
_____
_____
_____

Recipe Name: _____ **Serves:** _____

Ingredients:

_____	_____
_____	_____
_____	_____
_____	_____
_____	_____
_____	_____
_____	_____

Directions:

_____

_____

_____

_____

_____

_____

_____

_____

_____

_____

_____

_____

_____

Serving finger foods before dinner?
Offer small bites like marinated
olives that will pique guests'
appetites but not fill them up.

Recipe Name: _____   **Serves:** _____

Ingredients:

_____   _____

_____   _____

_____   _____

_____   _____

_____   _____

_____   _____

_____   _____

Directions:

_____

_____

_____

_____

_____

_____

_____

_____

_____

_____

_____

_____

_____

_____

_____

_____

_____

_____

Recipe Name: _____ **Serves:** _____

Ingredients:

_____   _____

_____   _____

_____   _____

_____   _____

_____   _____

_____   _____

_____

Directions:

_____

_____

_____

_____

_____

_____

_____

_____

_____

_____

_____

_____

_____

_____

_____

_____

_____

Appetizers

Recipe Name: _____ **Serves:** ____

Ingredients:

_____ _____
_____ _____
_____ _____
_____ _____
_____ _____
_____ _____
_____ _____

Directions:

_____
_____
_____
_____
_____
_____
_____
_____
_____
_____
_____
_____
_____
_____
_____

Have appetizers for dinner! Set up a family-size sampler with mozzarella sticks, mini pizza snacks, mini egg rolls, potato skins and a bunch of dippers to try too. Don't forget the French fries!

Recipe Name: _____ **Serves:** _____

Ingredients:

_____   _____
_____   _____
_____   _____
_____   _____
_____   _____
_____   _____

Directions:

_____
_____
_____
_____
_____
_____
_____
_____
_____
_____
_____
_____
_____
_____
_____
_____
_____
_____
_____

Recipe Name: _____ **Serves:** _____

Ingredients:

_____   _____
_____   _____
_____   _____
_____   _____
_____   _____
_____   _____
_____   _____

Directions:

_____
_____
_____
_____
_____
_____
_____
_____
_____
_____
_____
_____
_____
_____
_____
_____
_____
_____
_____

Recipe Name: _____ **Serves:** _____

Ingredients:

_____ _____

_____ _____

_____ _____

_____ _____

_____ _____

_____ _____

_____ _____

Directions:

_____

_____

_____

_____

_____

_____

_____

_____

_____

_____

_____

_____

_____

_____

_____

_____

_____

_____

_____

Appetizers

Recipe Name: _____ **Serves:** _____

Ingredients:

_____   _____
_____   _____
_____   _____
_____   _____
_____   _____
_____   _____
_____

Directions:

_____
_____
_____
_____
_____
_____
_____
_____
_____
_____
_____
_____
_____
_____
_____
_____
_____
_____

Recipe Name: _____ Serves: _____

Ingredients:

_____   _____

_____   _____

_____   _____

_____   _____

_____   _____

_____   _____

Directions:

_____

_____

_____

_____

_____

_____

_____

_____

_____

_____

_____

_____

Use tiny pretzel sticks instead of
toothpicks for spearing cheese cubes.

Recipe Name: _____   **Serves:** _____

Ingredients:

_____   _____
_____   _____
_____   _____
_____   _____
_____   _____
_____   _____
_____

Directions:

_____
_____
_____
_____
_____
_____
_____
_____
_____
_____
_____
_____
_____
_____
_____
_____
_____
_____

Recipe Name: _____ **Serves:** _____

Ingredients:

_____   _____

_____   _____

_____   _____

_____   _____

_____   _____

_____   _____

_____   _____

Directions:

_____

_____

_____

_____

_____

_____

_____

_____

_____

_____

_____

_____

_____

_____

_____

_____

_____

Appetizers

Recipe Name: _____ **Serves:** _____

Ingredients:

_____   _____
_____   _____
_____   _____
_____   _____
_____   _____
_____   _____
_____   _____

Directions:

_____
_____
_____
_____
_____
_____
_____
_____
_____
_____
_____
_____
_____
_____

Sour cream can be mixed with any of
the seasoning blends found at the meat
counter. Try some different blends for
an endless variety of savory dips!

Recipe Name: _____   **Serves:** _____

Ingredients:

_____   _____

_____   _____

_____   _____

_____   _____

_____   _____

_____   _____

_____

Directions:

_____

_____

_____

_____

_____

_____

_____

_____

_____

_____

_____

_____

_____

_____

_____

_____

_____

Recipe Name: _____   **Serves:** _____

Ingredients:

_____   _____

_____   _____

_____   _____

_____   _____

_____   _____

_____   _____

_____   _____

Directions:

_____

_____

_____

_____

_____

_____

_____

_____

_____

_____

_____

_____

_____

_____

_____

_____

_____

_____

Recipe Name: _____ **Serves:** _____

Ingredients:

_____ _____
_____ _____
_____ _____
_____ _____
_____ _____
_____ _____

Directions:

_____
_____
_____
_____
_____
_____
_____
_____
_____
_____
_____
_____
_____
_____
_____
_____
_____
_____

Recipe Name: _____ Serves: _____

Ingredients:

_____   _____
_____   _____
_____   _____
_____   _____
_____   _____
_____   _____
_____   _____

Directions:

_____
_____
_____
_____
_____
_____
_____
_____
_____
_____
_____
_____
_____
_____
_____
_____
_____
_____

Appetizers

Recipe Name: _____ **Serves:** _____

Ingredients:

_____   _____

_____   _____

_____   _____

_____   _____

_____   _____

_____   _____

_____   _____

Directions:

_____

_____

_____

_____

_____

_____

_____

_____

_____

_____

_____

_____

_____

_____

Appetizer spreads are perfect for enjoying during card games or a favorite movie at home with friends! Set out a variety of creamy dips, crunchy snacks and sweet munchies along with fizzy beverages.

Recipe Name: _____ **Serves:** _____

Ingredients:

_____   _____

_____   _____

_____   _____

_____   _____

_____   _____

_____   _____

_____

Directions:

_____

_____

_____

_____

_____

_____

_____

_____

_____

_____

_____

_____

_____

_____

_____

_____

_____

_____

_____

Recipe Name: _____ **Serves:** _____

Ingredients:

_____   _____

_____   _____

_____   _____

_____   _____

_____   _____

_____   _____

_____   _____

Directions:

_____

_____

_____

_____

_____

_____

_____

_____

_____

_____

_____

_____

_____

_____

_____

_____

_____

Recipe Name: _____ **Serves:** _____

Ingredients:

_____   _____
_____   _____
_____   _____
_____   _____
_____   _____
_____   _____
_____

Directions:

_____
_____
_____
_____
_____
_____
_____
_____
_____
_____
_____
_____
_____
_____
_____
_____

Making deviled eggs? Whip 'em up in no time by combining ingredients in a plastic zipping bag instead of a bowl. Blend by squeezing the bag, snip off a corner and pipe the filling into the whites...what could be easier?

Recipe Name: _____   **Serves:** _____

Ingredients:

_____   _____

_____   _____

_____   _____

_____   _____

_____   _____

_____   _____

_____

Directions:

_____

_____

_____

_____

_____

_____

_____

_____

_____

_____

_____

_____

_____

_____

_____

_____

_____

_____

Recipe Name: _____ **Serves:** _____

Ingredients:

_____   _____
_____   _____
_____   _____
_____   _____
_____   _____
_____   _____
_____   _____

Directions:

_____
_____
_____
_____
_____
_____
_____
_____
_____
_____
_____
_____
_____
_____
_____
_____
_____
_____

My Favorite
Soup & Bread
RECIPES

NOTES

_____

_____

_____

_____

_____

_____

_____

_____

Recipe Name: _____ **Serves:** _____

Ingredients:

_____ _____
_____ _____
_____ _____
_____ _____
_____ _____
_____ _____

Directions:

_____
_____
_____
_____
_____
_____
_____
_____
_____
_____
_____
_____
_____
_____
_____
_____
_____
_____
_____

Recipe Name: _____ **Serves:** _____

Ingredients:

_____   _____

_____   _____

_____   _____

_____   _____

_____   _____

_____   _____

_____   _____

Directions:

_____

_____

_____

_____

_____

_____

_____

_____

_____

_____

_____

_____

_____

_____

_____

_____

_____

Soups & Breads

Recipe Name: _____ **Serves:** _____

Ingredients:

_____   _____

_____   _____

_____   _____

_____   _____

_____   _____

_____   _____

_____   _____

Directions:

_____

_____

_____

_____

_____

_____

_____

_____

_____

_____

_____

_____

_____

_____

_____

_____

Serve your favorite chili recipe with a variety
of yummy toppings...sour cream, chives,
Cheddar cheese or hot peppers. Use cookie
cutters to cut squares of cornbread into fun
shapes for serving alongside your soup.

Recipe Name: _____ **Serves:** _____

Ingredients:

_____   _____

_____   _____

_____   _____

_____   _____

_____   _____

_____   _____

_____

Directions:

_____

_____

_____

_____

_____

_____

_____

_____

_____

_____

_____

_____

_____

_____

_____

_____

_____

_____

Recipe Name: _____ **Serves:** _____

Ingredients:

_____   _____

_____   _____

_____   _____

_____   _____

_____   _____

_____   _____

_____

Directions:

_____

_____

_____

_____

_____

_____

_____

_____

_____

_____

_____

_____

_____

_____

_____

_____

_____

_____

Soups & Breads

Recipe Name: _____ **Serves:** _____

Ingredients:

_____   _____

_____   _____

_____   _____

_____   _____

_____   _____

_____   _____

_____   _____

Directions:

_____

_____

_____

_____

_____

_____

_____

_____

_____

_____

_____

_____

_____

_____

_____

_____

Soups & Breads

Recipe Name: _____ **Serves:** _____

Ingredients:

_____   _____

_____   _____

_____   _____

_____   _____

_____   _____

_____   _____

Directions:

_____

_____

_____

_____

_____

_____

_____

_____

_____

_____

_____

_____

_____

_____

_____

_____

_____

_____

Soups & Breads

Recipe Name: _____ **Serves:** _____

Ingredients:

_____   _____

_____   _____

_____   _____

_____   _____

_____   _____

_____   _____

_____

Directions:

_____

_____

_____

_____

_____

_____

_____

_____

_____

_____

_____

_____

_____

_____

_____

To give your warm-from-the-oven bread
a sweet, shiny glaze, brush with
honey...it also absorbs moisture and
bread will stay fresh longer.

Recipe Name: _____ Serves: _____

Ingredients:

_____ _____

_____ _____

_____ _____

_____ _____

_____ _____

_____ _____

_____

Directions:

_____

_____

_____

_____

_____

_____

_____

_____

_____

_____

_____

_____

_____

_____

_____

_____

_____

Recipe Name: _____ **Serves:** _____

Ingredients:

_____ _____

_____ _____

_____ _____

_____ _____

_____ _____

_____ _____

Directions:

_____

_____

_____

_____

_____

_____

_____

_____

_____

_____

_____

_____

_____

_____

_____

_____

_____

Soups & Breads

Recipe Name: _____ **Serves:** _____

Ingredients:

_____   _____

_____   _____

_____   _____

_____   _____

_____   _____

_____   _____

Directions:

_____

_____

_____

_____

_____

_____

_____

_____

_____

_____

_____

_____

_____

_____

Homemade chicken broth is simple to make. Whenever you boil chicken for a recipe, save the broth and freeze it. When it's time to make broth, thaw and combine with desired amount of chopped onion, chopped carrots and sliced celery. Simmer, uncovered, for an hour and strain if desired.

Recipe Name: _____ **Serves:** _____

Ingredients:

_____   _____
_____   _____
_____   _____
_____   _____
_____   _____
_____   _____
_____   _____

Directions:

_____
_____
_____
_____
_____
_____
_____
_____
_____
_____
_____
_____
_____
_____
_____
_____
_____
_____

Recipe Name: _____ **Serves:** _____

Ingredients:

_____   _____
_____   _____
_____   _____
_____   _____
_____   _____
_____   _____

Directions:

_____
_____
_____
_____
_____
_____
_____
_____
_____
_____
_____
_____
_____
_____
_____
_____
_____
_____

Recipe Name: _____   **Serves:** _____

Ingredients:

_____   _____

_____   _____

_____   _____

_____   _____

_____   _____

_____   _____

Directions:

_____

_____

_____

_____

_____

_____

_____

_____

_____

_____

_____

_____

_____

_____

_____

_____

_____

_____

Soups & Breads

Recipe Name: _____ **Serves:** _____

Ingredients:

_____   _____

_____   _____

_____   _____

_____   _____

_____   _____

_____   _____

_____   _____

Directions:

_____

_____

_____

_____

_____

_____

_____

_____

_____

_____

_____

_____

_____

_____

_____

_____

_____

_____

_____

_____

_____

_____

Recipe Name: _____ **Serves:** _____

Ingredients:

_____   _____
_____   _____
_____   _____
_____   _____
_____   _____
_____   _____

Directions:

_____
_____
_____
_____
_____
_____
_____
_____
_____
_____
_____
_____
_____
_____

Tea towels from the 1940's are perfect bread basket liners and add a splash of color to any table.

Recipe Name: _____ **Serves:** _____

Ingredients:

_____   _____
_____   _____
_____   _____
_____   _____
_____   _____
_____   _____
_____   _____

Directions:

_____
_____
_____
_____
_____
_____
_____
_____
_____
_____
_____
_____
_____
_____
_____
_____
_____
_____

Soups & Breads

Recipe Name: _____ **Serves:** _____

Ingredients:

_____   _____

_____   _____

_____   _____

_____   _____

_____   _____

_____   _____

_____   _____

Directions:

_____

_____

_____

_____

_____

_____

_____

_____

_____

_____

_____

_____

_____

_____

_____

_____

_____

_____

Soups & Breads

Recipe Name: _____   **Serves:** _____

Ingredients:

_____   _____
_____   _____
_____   _____
_____   _____
_____   _____
_____   _____
_____

Directions:

_____
_____
_____
_____
_____
_____
_____
_____
_____
_____
_____
_____
_____
_____
_____
_____
_____

Thicken vegetable soup with a sprinkling
of instant mashed potato flakes...just right
for warming up on a chilly afternoon.

Recipe Name: _____ **Serves:** _____

Ingredients:

_____   _____
_____   _____
_____   _____
_____   _____
_____   _____
_____   _____
_____   _____

Directions:

_____
_____
_____
_____
_____
_____
_____
_____
_____
_____
_____
_____
_____
_____
_____
_____
_____

Soups & Breads

Recipe Name: _____ **Serves:** _____

Ingredients:

_____   _____

_____   _____

_____   _____

_____   _____

_____   _____

_____   _____

Directions:

_____

_____

_____

_____

_____

_____

_____

_____

_____

_____

_____

_____

_____

_____

_____

_____

_____

_____

Soups & Breads

My Favorite
Side & Salad
RECIPES

NOTES

_____

_____

_____

_____

_____

_____

_____

_____

_____

Recipe Name: _____ **Serves:** _____

Ingredients:

_____   _____

_____   _____

_____   _____

_____   _____

_____   _____

_____   _____

Directions:

_____

_____

_____

_____

_____

_____

_____

_____

_____

_____

_____

_____

_____

_____

_____

_____

_____

_____

_____

Sides & Salads

Recipe Name: _____ **Serves:** _____

Ingredients:

_____   _____

_____   _____

_____   _____

_____   _____

_____   _____

_____   _____

_____

Directions:

_____

_____

_____

_____

_____

_____

_____

_____

_____

_____

_____

_____

_____

_____

_____

_____

_____

Sides & Salads

Recipe Name: _____ **Serves:** _____

Ingredients:

_____   _____

_____   _____

_____   _____

_____   _____

_____   _____

_____   _____

Directions:

_____

_____

_____

_____

_____

_____

_____

_____

_____

_____

_____

_____

_____

_____

Red-ripe tomatoes make delicious salad bowls. Cut a slice from the top of the tomato and use a spoon to scoop out the seeds. Cut the tomato edge into scallops or a zig-zag pattern, sprinkle with salt, invert on paper towels and chill. Fill right before serving.

Recipe Name: _____ **Serves:** _____

Ingredients:

_____   _____

_____   _____

_____   _____

_____   _____

_____   _____

_____   _____

_____   _____

Directions:

_____

_____

_____

_____

_____

_____

_____

_____

_____

_____

_____

_____

_____

_____

_____

_____

_____

Sides & Salads

Recipe Name: _____ **Serves:** _____

Ingredients:

_____   _____

_____   _____

_____   _____

_____   _____

_____   _____

_____   _____

Directions:

_____

_____

_____

_____

_____

_____

_____

_____

_____

_____

_____

_____

_____

_____

_____

_____

_____

_____

Sides & Salads

Recipe Name: _____   **Serves:** _____

Ingredients:

_____   _____

_____   _____

_____   _____

_____   _____

_____   _____

_____   _____

_____

Directions:

_____

_____

_____

_____

_____

_____

_____

_____

_____

_____

_____

_____

_____

_____

_____

_____

_____

Sides & Salads

Recipe Name: _____ Serves: _____

Ingredients:

_____   _____
_____   _____
_____   _____
_____   _____
_____   _____
_____   _____
_____   _____

Directions:

_____
_____
_____
_____
_____
_____
_____
_____
_____
_____
_____
_____
_____
_____
_____
_____
_____
_____
_____

Recipe Name: _____ **Serves:** _____

Ingredients:

_____   _____
_____   _____
_____   _____
_____   _____
_____   _____
_____   _____
_____

Directions:

_____
_____
_____
_____
_____
_____
_____
_____
_____
_____
_____
_____
_____
_____

For a really quick side dish, cook chopped green peppers in butter for about 5 minutes. Add canned corn and salt and simmer until golden...yummy.

Recipe Name: _____ **Serves:** _____

Ingredients:

_____   _____
_____   _____
_____   _____
_____   _____
_____   _____
_____   _____
_____

Directions:

_____
_____
_____
_____
_____
_____
_____
_____
_____
_____
_____
_____
_____
_____
_____
_____
_____
_____
_____

Recipe Name: _____ **Serves:** _____

Ingredients:

_____   _____

_____   _____

_____   _____

_____   _____

_____   _____

_____   _____

_____   _____

Directions:

_____

_____

_____

_____

_____

_____

_____

_____

_____

_____

_____

_____

_____

_____

_____

_____

_____

Sides & Salads

Recipe Name: _____ **Serves:** _____

Ingredients:

_____   _____

_____   _____

_____   _____

_____   _____

_____   _____

_____   _____

_____   _____

Directions:

_____

_____

_____

_____

_____

_____

_____

_____

_____

_____

_____

_____

_____

_____

_____

Add a pinch of sugar to the water when boiling ears of fresh summer corn...it'll bring out its natural sweetness.

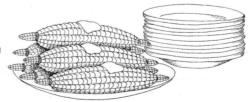

Recipe Name: _____ **Serves:** _____

Ingredients:

_____   _____

_____   _____

_____   _____

_____   _____

_____   _____

_____   _____

Directions:

_____

_____

_____

_____

_____

_____

_____

_____

_____

_____

_____

_____

_____

_____

_____

_____

_____

_____

Recipe Name: _____ Serves: _____

Ingredients:

_____   _____
_____   _____
_____   _____
_____   _____
_____   _____
_____   _____

Directions:

_____
_____
_____
_____
_____
_____
_____
_____
_____
_____
_____
_____
_____
_____
_____
_____
_____
_____
_____

Recipe Name: _____   **Serves:** _____

Ingredients:

_____   _____
_____   _____
_____   _____
_____   _____
_____   _____
_____   _____
_____   _____

Directions:

_____
_____
_____
_____
_____
_____
_____
_____
_____
_____
_____
_____
_____
_____
_____
_____
_____
_____

Sides & Salads

Recipe Name: _____   **Serves:** _____

Ingredients:

_____   _____

_____   _____

_____   _____

_____   _____

_____   _____

_____   _____

Directions:

_____

_____

_____

_____

_____

_____

_____

_____

_____

_____

_____

_____

_____

_____

_____

_____

_____

Sides & Salads

Recipe Name: _____ **Serves:** _____

Ingredients:

_____   _____

_____   _____

_____   _____

_____   _____

_____   _____

_____   _____

Directions:

_____

_____

_____

_____

_____

_____

_____

_____

_____

_____

_____

_____

_____

_____

Pasta salad is so versatile and works well with just about any veggies on hand. Toss chopped celery, cucumbers, grated carrots or even cheese chunks in for a new dish every time.

Recipe Name: _____ **Serves:** _____

Ingredients:

_____   _____
_____   _____
_____   _____
_____   _____
_____   _____
_____   _____

Directions:

_____
_____
_____
_____
_____
_____
_____
_____
_____
_____
_____
_____
_____
_____
_____
_____
_____
_____

Sides & Salads

Recipe Name: _____   **Serves:** _____

Ingredients:

_____   _____

_____   _____

_____   _____

_____   _____

_____   _____

_____   _____

_____

Directions:

_____

_____

_____

_____

_____

_____

_____

_____

_____

_____

_____

_____

_____

_____

_____

_____

_____

Sides & Salads

Recipe Name: _____   **Serves:** _____

Ingredients:

_____   _____

_____   _____

_____   _____

_____   _____

_____   _____

_____   _____

_____   _____

Directions:

_____

_____

_____

_____

_____

_____

_____

_____

_____

_____

_____

_____

_____

_____

Cook a double batch of rice, then freeze half
in a plastic freezer bag for another meal.
When you're ready to use the frozen rice,
just microwave on high for one minute per cup
to thaw, 2 to 3 minutes per cup to warm it
through. Fluff with a fork...ready to use!

Recipe Name: _____ **Serves:** _____

Ingredients:

_____ _____
_____ _____
_____ _____
_____ _____
_____ _____
_____ _____
_____

Directions:

_____
_____
_____
_____
_____
_____
_____
_____
_____
_____
_____
_____
_____
_____
_____
_____
_____

Sides & Salads

Recipe Name: _____ Serves: _____

Ingredients:

_____   _____
_____   _____
_____   _____
_____   _____
_____   _____
_____   _____
_____   _____

Directions:

_____
_____
_____
_____
_____
_____
_____
_____
_____
_____
_____
_____
_____
_____
_____
_____
_____
_____
_____

Sides & Salads

My Favorite
Main Dish
RECIPES

NOTES

_____

_____

_____

_____

_____

_____

_____

_____

_____

Recipe Name: _____ **Serves:** _____

Ingredients:

_____ _____

_____ _____

_____ _____

_____ _____

_____ _____

_____ _____

_____ _____

Directions:

_____

_____

_____

_____

_____

_____

_____

_____

_____

_____

_____

_____

_____

_____

_____

_____

_____

_____

_____

_____

Recipe Name: _____   **Serves:** _____

Ingredients:

_____   _____

_____   _____

_____   _____

_____   _____

_____   _____

_____   _____

Directions:

_____

_____

_____

_____

_____

_____

_____

_____

_____

_____

_____

_____

_____

_____

_____

_____

_____

_____

Main Dishes

Recipe Name: _____ **Serves:** _____

Ingredients:

_____   _____
_____   _____
_____   _____
_____   _____
_____   _____
_____   _____

Directions:

_____
_____
_____
_____
_____
_____
_____
_____
_____
_____
_____
_____
_____
_____

Keep browned ground beef on hand for easy
meal prep. Crumble several pounds of beef
into a baking pan and bake at 350 degrees
until browned through, stirring often. Drain
well and pack recipe portions in freezer bags.

Recipe Name: _____ **Serves:** _____

Ingredients:

_____   _____

_____   _____

_____   _____

_____   _____

_____   _____

_____   _____

_____

Directions:

_____

_____

_____

_____

_____

_____

_____

_____

_____

_____

_____

_____

_____

_____

_____

_____

_____

_____

Main Dishes

Recipe Name: _____ Serves: _____

Ingredients:

_____   _____

_____   _____

_____   _____

_____   _____

_____   _____

_____   _____

_____   _____

Directions:

_____

_____

_____

_____

_____

_____

_____

_____

_____

_____

_____

_____

_____

_____

_____

_____

_____

Main Dishes

Recipe Name: _____ **Serves:** _____

Ingredients:

_____ _____

_____ _____

_____ _____

_____ _____

_____ _____

_____ _____

_____

Directions:

_____

_____

_____

_____

_____

_____

_____

_____

_____

_____

_____

_____

_____

_____

_____

_____

_____

_____

_____

Main Dishes

Recipe Name: _____ **Serves:** _____

Ingredients:

_____   _____

_____   _____

_____   _____

_____   _____

_____   _____

_____   _____

_____

Directions:

_____

_____

_____

_____

_____

_____

_____

_____

_____

_____

_____

_____

_____

_____

_____

_____

_____

Recipe Name: _____ **Serves:** _____

Ingredients:

_____   _____

_____   _____

_____   _____

_____   _____

_____   _____

_____   _____

_____

Directions:

_____

_____

_____

_____

_____

_____

_____

_____

_____

_____

_____

_____

_____

_____

_____

_____

Making your favorite casserole? Make
an extra to freeze. Enjoy the next time
you need a quick dinner!

Recipe Name: _____ **Serves:** _____

Ingredients:

_____   _____

_____   _____

_____   _____

_____   _____

_____   _____

Directions:

_____

_____

_____

_____

_____

_____

_____

_____

_____

_____

_____

_____

_____

_____

_____

_____

_____

_____

_____

Main Dishes

Recipe Name: _____ **Serves:** _____

Ingredients:

_____   _____

_____   _____

_____   _____

_____   _____

_____   _____

_____   _____

_____

Directions:

_____

_____

_____

_____

_____

_____

_____

_____

_____

_____

_____

_____

_____

_____

_____

_____

_____

_____

Main Dishes

Recipe Name: _____ **Serves:** _____

Ingredients:

_____   _____
_____   _____
_____   _____
_____   _____
_____   _____
_____   _____

Directions:

_____
_____
_____
_____
_____
_____
_____
_____
_____
_____
_____
_____
_____

An easy way to beef up any recipe...crumble leftover meatloaf or cut roast beef into bite-size pieces, season to taste and toss into casseroles, soups and sauces.

Recipe Name: _____ **Serves:** _____

Ingredients:

_____   _____

_____   _____

_____   _____

_____   _____

_____   _____

_____   _____

Directions:

_____

_____

_____

_____

_____

_____

_____

_____

_____

_____

_____

_____

_____

_____

_____

_____

_____

_____

Main Dishes

Recipe Name: _____ **Serves:** _____

Ingredients:

_____   _____

_____   _____

_____   _____

_____   _____

_____   _____

_____   _____

_____

Directions:

_____

_____

_____

_____

_____

_____

_____

_____

_____

_____

_____

_____

_____

_____

_____

_____

_____

_____

Recipe Name: _____ **Serves:** _____

Ingredients:

_____ _____
_____ _____
_____ _____
_____ _____
_____ _____
_____ _____
_____ _____

Directions:

_____
_____
_____
_____
_____
_____
_____
_____
_____
_____
_____
_____
_____
_____
_____
_____
_____
_____

Main Dishes

Recipe Name: _____ **Serves:** _____

Ingredients:

_____   _____

_____   _____

_____   _____

_____   _____

_____   _____

_____   _____

Directions:

_____

_____

_____

_____

_____

_____

_____

_____

_____

_____

_____

_____

_____

_____

_____

_____

_____

_____

Recipe Name: _____ **Serves:** _____

Ingredients:

_____   _____

_____   _____

_____   _____

_____   _____

_____   _____

_____   _____

_____   _____

Directions:

_____

_____

_____

_____

_____

_____

_____

_____

_____

_____

_____

_____

_____

_____

Casseroles really taste better if they're made
in advance to allow the flavors to blend.
Make one the night before, then pop in the
oven to bake the next day for dinner.

Recipe Name: _____ **Serves:** _____

Ingredients:

_____	_____
_____	_____
_____	_____
_____	_____
_____	_____
_____	_____

Directions:

_____

_____

_____

_____

_____

_____

_____

_____

_____

_____

_____

_____

_____

_____

_____

_____

_____

Main Dishes

Recipe Name: _____ **Serves:** _____

Ingredients:

_____   _____
_____   _____
_____   _____
_____   _____
_____   _____
_____   _____

Directions:

_____
_____
_____
_____
_____
_____
_____
_____
_____
_____
_____
_____
_____
_____
_____
_____
_____
_____
_____

Recipe Name: _____ **Serves:** _____

Ingredients:

_____   _____
_____   _____
_____   _____
_____   _____
_____   _____
_____   _____
_____   _____

Directions:

_____
_____
_____
_____
_____
_____
_____
_____
_____
_____
_____
_____
_____
_____
_____

Potluck dinners are a wonderful way to share food and fellowship with friends. Why not make a standing date once a month to try new recipes as well as tried & true favorites?

Recipe Name: _____ **Serves:** _____

Ingredients:

_____   _____

_____   _____

_____   _____

_____   _____

_____   _____

_____   _____

_____   _____

Directions:

_____

_____

_____

_____

_____

_____

_____

_____

_____

_____

_____

_____

_____

_____

_____

_____

_____

Main Dishes

Recipe Name: _____ **Serves:** _____

Ingredients:

_____   _____

_____   _____

_____   _____

_____   _____

_____   _____

_____   _____

Directions:

_____

_____

_____

_____

_____

_____

_____

_____

_____

_____

_____

_____

_____

_____

_____

_____

_____

_____

Main Dishes

Recipe Name: _____ **Serves:** _____

Ingredients:

_____   _____

_____   _____

_____   _____

_____   _____

_____   _____

_____   _____

Directions:

_____

_____

_____

_____

_____

_____

_____

_____

_____

_____

_____

_____

_____

_____

_____

_____

_____

_____

_____

Recipe Name: _____ **Serves:** _____

Ingredients:

_____   _____
_____   _____
_____   _____
_____   _____
_____   _____
_____   _____

Directions:

_____
_____
_____
_____
_____
_____
_____
_____
_____
_____
_____
_____
_____
_____
_____
_____
_____
_____

Recipe Name: _____   **Serves:** _____

Ingredients:

_____   _____

_____   _____

_____   _____

_____   _____

_____   _____

_____   _____

_____   _____

Directions:

_____

_____

_____

_____

_____

_____

_____

_____

_____

_____

_____

_____

_____

Hot! Hot! If a dish turns out spicier
than you expected, turn down the heat
by stirring in a tablespoon each of sugar
and lemon or lime juice.

Recipe Name: _____ **Serves:** _____

Ingredients:

_____   _____

_____   _____

_____   _____

_____   _____

_____   _____

_____   _____

Directions:

_____

_____

_____

_____

_____

_____

_____

_____

_____

_____

_____

_____

_____

_____

_____

_____

_____

_____

Main Dishes

Recipe Name: _____ **Serves:** _____

Ingredients:

_____   _____

_____   _____

_____   _____

_____   _____

_____   _____

_____   _____

Directions:

_____

_____

_____

_____

_____

_____

_____

_____

_____

_____

_____

_____

_____

_____

_____

_____

_____

_____

Main Dishes

Recipe Name: _____   **Serves:** _____

Ingredients:

_____   _____
_____   _____
_____   _____
_____   _____
_____   _____
_____   _____
_____   _____

Directions:

_____
_____
_____
_____
_____
_____
_____
_____
_____
_____
_____
_____
_____
_____

No peeking! When baking, every time
the oven door is open, the temperature
drops 25 degrees.

Recipe Name: _____ **Serves:** _____

Ingredients:

_____   _____

_____   _____

_____   _____

_____   _____

_____   _____

_____   _____

_____   _____

Directions:

_____

_____

_____

_____

_____

_____

_____

_____

_____

_____

_____

_____

_____

_____

_____

_____

_____

_____

Main Dishes

Recipe Name: _____   **Serves:** _____

Ingredients:

_____   _____

_____   _____

_____   _____

_____   _____

_____   _____

_____   _____

Directions:

_____

_____

_____

_____

_____

_____

_____

_____

_____

_____

_____

_____

_____

_____

_____

_____

_____

My Favorite
Dessert
RECIPES

NOTES

_____

_____

_____

_____

_____

_____

_____

_____

_____

Recipe Name: _____   **Serves:** _____

Ingredients:

_____   _____

_____   _____

_____   _____

_____   _____

_____   _____

_____   _____

_____   _____

Directions:

_____

_____

_____

_____

_____

_____

_____

_____

_____

_____

_____

_____

_____

_____

_____

_____

_____

_____

Recipe Name: _____ **Serves:** _____

Ingredients:

_____   _____

_____   _____

_____   _____

_____   _____

_____   _____

Directions:

_____

_____

_____

_____

_____

_____

_____

_____

_____

_____

_____

_____

_____

_____

Why save pie just for dessert? Invite family
& friends for a pie social...everyone brings
their favorite pie, and you provide the
ice cream and whipped topping.

Recipe Name: _____ Serves: _____

Ingredients:

_____   _____
_____   _____
_____   _____
_____   _____
_____   _____
_____   _____
_____

Directions:

_____
_____
_____
_____
_____
_____
_____
_____
_____
_____
_____
_____
_____
_____
_____
_____
_____
_____
_____

Recipe Name: _____ **Serves:** _____

Ingredients:

_____ _____

_____ _____

_____ _____

_____ _____

_____ _____

_____ _____

_____

Directions:

_____

_____

_____

_____

_____

_____

_____

_____

_____

_____

_____

_____

_____

_____

_____

_____

_____

_____

_____

Recipe Name: _____ **Serves:** _____

Ingredients:

_____   _____
_____   _____
_____   _____
_____   _____
_____   _____
_____   _____
_____   _____

Directions:

_____
_____
_____
_____
_____
_____
_____
_____
_____
_____
_____
_____
_____
_____
_____

Make your favorite hot chocolate extra special
by adding a scoop of vanilla ice cream. Then top
with whipped cream and dust with cocoa powder.
Add a cinnamon stick and sprinkle some
chocolate curls on top. Totally yummy!

Recipe Name: _____ **Serves:** _____

Ingredients:

_____   _____
_____   _____
_____   _____
_____   _____
_____   _____
_____   _____
_____   _____

Directions:

_____
_____
_____
_____
_____
_____
_____
_____
_____
_____
_____
_____
_____
_____
_____
_____
_____
_____
_____

Recipe Name: _____ **Serves:** _____

Ingredients:

_____   _____
_____   _____
_____   _____
_____   _____
_____   _____
_____   _____
_____

Directions:

_____
_____
_____
_____
_____
_____
_____
_____
_____
_____
_____
_____
_____
_____
_____
_____
_____
_____
_____

Recipe Name: _____ **Serves:** _____

Ingredients:

_____   _____

_____   _____

_____   _____

_____   _____

_____   _____

_____   _____

Directions:

_____

_____

_____

_____

_____

_____

_____

_____

_____

_____

_____

_____

_____

_____

_____

_____

_____

_____

_____

Recipe Name: _____ **Serves:** _____

Ingredients:

_____   _____

_____   _____

_____   _____

_____   _____

_____   _____

_____   _____

Directions:

_____

_____

_____

_____

_____

_____

_____

_____

_____

_____

_____

_____

_____

_____

_____

_____

Recipe Name: _____ **Serves:** _____

Ingredients:

_____   _____

_____   _____

_____   _____

_____   _____

_____   _____

_____

Directions:

_____

_____

_____

_____

_____

_____

_____

_____

_____

_____

_____

_____

_____

_____

_____

_____

Does a pie recipe say to dot the filling with butter?
Just run a vegetable peeler over a frozen stick
of butter...less mess!

Recipe Name: _____ **Serves:** _____

Ingredients:

_____   _____
_____   _____
_____   _____
_____   _____
_____   _____
_____   _____
_____   _____

Directions:

_____
_____
_____
_____
_____
_____
_____
_____
_____
_____
_____
_____
_____
_____
_____
_____

Desserts

Recipe Name: _____ **Serves:** _____

Ingredients:

_____   _____
_____   _____
_____   _____
_____   _____
_____   _____
_____   _____
_____   _____

Directions:

_____
_____
_____
_____
_____
_____
_____
_____
_____
_____
_____
_____
_____
_____
_____
_____
_____
_____
_____

Recipe Name: _____   **Serves:** _____

Ingredients:

_____   _____

_____   _____

_____   _____

_____   _____

_____   _____

_____   _____

Directions:

_____

_____

_____

_____

_____

_____

_____

_____

_____

_____

_____

_____

_____

_____

For a guaranteed crumb-free frosting, add a very
thin layer of frosting to a cake and refrigerate.
When the frosting is firm, go ahead, frost and
decorate as desired...it'll be beautiful!

Recipe Name: _____ **Serves:** _____

Ingredients:

_____   _____

_____   _____

_____   _____

_____   _____

_____   _____

_____   _____

Directions:

_____

_____

_____

_____

_____

_____

_____

_____

_____

_____

_____

_____

_____

_____

_____

_____

_____

_____

Recipe Name: _____ **Serves:** _____

Ingredients:

_____   _____
_____   _____
_____   _____
_____   _____
_____   _____
_____   _____

Directions:

_____
_____
_____
_____
_____
_____
_____
_____
_____
_____
_____
_____
_____
_____
_____
_____
_____
_____
_____

Recipe Name: _____ **Serves:** _____

Ingredients:

_____   _____
_____   _____
_____   _____
_____   _____
_____   _____
_____   _____
_____

Directions:

_____
_____
_____
_____
_____
_____
_____
_____
_____
_____
_____
_____
_____
_____
_____
_____
_____
_____

Recipe Name: _____ **Serves:** _____

Ingredients:

_____   _____

_____   _____

_____   _____

_____   _____

_____   _____

_____   _____

_____

Directions:

_____

_____

_____

_____

_____

_____

_____

_____

_____

_____

_____

_____

_____

_____

_____

_____

_____

_____

Recipe Name: _____ **Serves:** _____

Ingredients:

_____   _____
_____   _____
_____   _____
_____   _____
_____   _____
_____   _____
_____

Directions:

_____
_____
_____
_____
_____
_____
_____
_____
_____
_____
_____
_____
_____

Removing honey from measuring cups or spoons has never been easier...just coat your spoon or cup with non-stick vegetable spray before measuring the honey.

Recipe Name: _____ **Serves:** _____

Ingredients:

_____   _____

_____   _____

_____   _____

_____   _____

_____   _____

_____   _____

_____   _____

Directions:

_____

_____

_____

_____

_____

_____

_____

_____

_____

_____

_____

_____

_____

_____

_____

_____

_____

_____

_____

Recipe Name: _____ **Serves:** _____

Ingredients:

_____   _____
_____   _____
_____   _____
_____   _____
_____   _____
_____   _____
_____   _____

Directions:

_____
_____
_____
_____
_____
_____
_____
_____
_____
_____
_____
_____
_____
_____
_____
_____

Recipe Name: _____ **Serves:** _____

Ingredients:

_____   _____

_____   _____

_____   _____

_____   _____

_____   _____

_____   _____

_____   _____

Directions:

_____

_____

_____

_____

_____

_____

_____

_____

_____

_____

_____

_____

_____

_____

_____

Make your own delicious frosty fruit pops...it's easy! Slice your favorite fruit and combine with fresh juice. Pour into small cups and set in the freezer. When partially frozen, insert popsicle sticks, then freeze until firm.

Recipe Name: _____ **Serves:** _____

Ingredients:

_____   _____

_____   _____

_____   _____

_____   _____

_____   _____

_____   _____

Directions:

_____

_____

_____

_____

_____

_____

_____

_____

_____

_____

_____

_____

_____

_____

_____

_____

_____

_____

Recipe Name: _____ **Serves:** _____

Ingredients:

_____   _____

_____   _____

_____   _____

_____   _____

_____   _____

_____   _____

Directions:

_____

_____

_____

_____

_____

_____

_____

_____

_____

_____

_____

_____

_____

_____

_____

_____

_____

_____

Recipe Name: _____ **Serves:** _____

Ingredients:

_____   _____

_____   _____

_____   _____

_____   _____

_____   _____

_____   _____

_____

Directions:

_____

_____

_____

_____

_____

_____

_____

_____

_____

_____

_____

_____

_____

_____

_____

_____

_____

_____

_____

Recipe Name: _____   **Serves:** _____

Ingredients:

_____   _____
_____   _____
_____   _____
_____   _____
_____   _____
_____   _____

Directions:

_____
_____
_____
_____
_____
_____
_____
_____
_____
_____
_____
_____
_____
_____
_____
_____
_____
_____
_____

Recipe Name: _____   **Serves:** _____

Ingredients:

_____   _____

_____   _____

_____   _____

_____   _____

_____   _____

_____   _____

_____

Directions:

_____

_____

_____

_____

_____

_____

_____

_____

_____

_____

_____

_____

_____

_____

Blend chocolate milk, a scoop of ice cream and
a spoonful of peanut butter to make a quick
and delicious milkshake in minutes.

Recipe Name: _____   **Serves:** _____

Ingredients:

_____   _____

_____   _____

_____   _____

_____   _____

_____   _____

_____   _____

Directions:

_____

_____

_____

_____

_____

_____

_____

_____

_____

_____

_____

_____

_____

_____

_____

_____

_____

_____

Recipe Name: _____ **Serves:** _____

Ingredients:

_____   _____
_____   _____
_____   _____
_____   _____
_____   _____
_____   _____
_____   _____

Directions:

_____
_____
_____
_____
_____
_____
_____
_____
_____
_____
_____
_____
_____
_____
_____
_____
_____
_____

Recipe Name: _____ **Serves:** _____

Ingredients:

_____   _____
_____   _____
_____   _____
_____   _____
_____   _____
_____   _____
_____   _____

Directions:

_____
_____
_____
_____
_____
_____
_____
_____
_____
_____
_____
_____
_____
_____
_____

A Grandma-style treat...roll out extra pie dough,
cut into strips and sprinkle with cinnamon-sugar.
Bake at 350 degrees until golden.

My Favorite

RECIPES

NOTES

_____

_____

_____

_____

_____

_____

_____

_____

_____

Recipe Name: _____ **Serves:** _____

Ingredients:

_____   _____

_____   _____

_____   _____

_____   _____

_____   _____

_____   _____

_____   _____

Directions:

_____

_____

_____

_____

_____

_____

_____

_____

_____

_____

_____

_____

_____

_____

_____

_____

_____

_____

Recipe Name: _____ **Serves:** _____

Ingredients:

_____   _____

_____   _____

_____   _____

_____   _____

_____   _____

_____   _____

_____

Directions:

_____

_____

_____

_____

_____

_____

_____

_____

_____

_____

_____

_____

_____

_____

_____

_____

_____

_____

_____

Recipe Name: _____ **Serves:** _____

Ingredients:

_____   _____

_____   _____

_____   _____

_____   _____

_____   _____

_____   _____

Directions:

_____

_____

_____

_____

_____

_____

_____

_____

_____

_____

_____

_____

_____

_____

Pretty name tags let everyone know
what beverages are being served.
Cut out card stock using whimsical
decorative-edge scissors, then tie on
with raffia or colorful rick-rack.

LEMONADE

APPLE CIDER

ICED TEA

Recipe Name: _____   **Serves:** _____

Ingredients:

_____   _____

_____   _____

_____   _____

_____   _____

_____   _____

_____   _____

_____

Directions:

_____

_____

_____

_____

_____

_____

_____

_____

_____

_____

_____

_____

_____

_____

_____

_____

_____

_____

Recipe Name: _____ **Serves:** _____

Ingredients:

_____ _____

_____ _____

_____ _____

_____ _____

_____ _____

_____ _____

_____

Directions:

_____

_____

_____

_____

_____

_____

_____

_____

_____

_____

_____

_____

_____

_____

_____

_____

_____

_____

Recipe Name: _____ **Serves:** _____

Ingredients:

_____   _____

_____   _____

_____   _____

_____   _____

_____   _____

_____   _____

_____   _____

Directions:

_____

_____

_____

_____

_____

_____

_____

_____

_____

_____

_____

_____

_____

_____

_____

_____

_____

_____

Recipe Name: _____ **Serves:** _____

Ingredients:

_____ _____
_____ _____
_____ _____
_____ _____
_____ _____
_____ _____

Directions:

_____
_____
_____
_____
_____
_____
_____
_____
_____
_____
_____
_____
_____
_____
_____
_____
_____
_____

Recipe Name: _____   Serves: _____

Ingredients:

_____   _____
_____   _____
_____   _____
_____   _____
_____   _____
_____   _____
_____   _____

Directions:

_____
_____
_____
_____
_____
_____
_____
_____
_____
_____
_____
_____
_____
_____

Animal crackers and cocoa to drink. That is
the finest of suppers, I think. When I'm grown
up and can have what I please, I think I shall
always insist up on these.
- Christopher Morley

Recipe Name: _____ **Serves:** _____

Ingredients:

_____   _____

_____   _____

_____   _____

_____   _____

_____   _____

_____   _____

_____   _____

Directions:

_____

_____

_____

_____

_____

_____

_____

_____

_____

_____

_____

_____

_____

_____

_____

_____

_____

_____

_____

Recipe Name: _____   **Serves:** _____

Ingredients:

_____   _____

_____   _____

_____   _____

_____   _____

_____   _____

_____   _____

_____   _____

Directions:

_____

_____

_____

_____

_____

_____

_____

_____

_____

_____

_____

_____

_____

_____

_____

_____

_____

_____

Recipe Name: _____ **Serves:** _____

Ingredients:

_____   _____

_____   _____

_____   _____

_____   _____

_____   _____

_____   _____

_____   _____

Directions:

_____

_____

_____

_____

_____

_____

_____

_____

_____

_____

_____

_____

_____

_____

For the quickest-ever candlelit
atmosphere, set several lighted tea lights
on the table and top them with metal
cheese graters. They'll cast the same
twinkling glow as pierced tin lanterns.

Recipe Name: _____ **Serves:** _____

Ingredients:

_____   _____

_____   _____

_____   _____

_____   _____

_____   _____

_____   _____

_____

Directions:

_____

_____

_____

_____

_____

_____

_____

_____

_____

_____

_____

_____

_____

_____

_____

_____

_____

_____

Recipe Name: _____ **Serves:** _____

Ingredients:

_____   _____

_____   _____

_____   _____

_____   _____

_____   _____

_____   _____

_____   _____

Directions:

_____

_____

_____

_____

_____

_____

_____

_____

_____

_____

_____

_____

_____

_____

_____

_____

_____

_____

Recipe Name: _____   **Serves:** _____

Ingredients:

_____   _____

_____   _____

_____   _____

_____   _____

_____   _____

_____   _____

_____   _____

Directions:

_____

_____

_____

_____

_____

_____

_____

_____

_____

_____

_____

_____

_____

_____

_____

_____

_____

_____

Recipe Name: _____ **Serves:** _____

Ingredients:

_____ _____

_____ _____

_____ _____

_____ _____

_____ _____

_____ _____

_____ _____

Directions:

_____

_____

_____

_____

_____

_____

_____

_____

_____

_____

_____

_____

_____

_____

_____

_____

_____

_____

_____

Recipe Name: _____   **Serves:** _____

Ingredients:

_____   _____
_____   _____
_____   _____
_____   _____
_____   _____
_____   _____

Directions:

_____
_____
_____
_____
_____
_____
_____
_____
_____
_____
_____
_____
_____
_____

Get out your slow cooker today...there's nothing like coming home to the aroma of dinner just waiting to be served!

Recipe Name: _____ **Serves:** _____

Ingredients:

_____   _____

_____   _____

_____   _____

_____   _____

_____   _____

_____   _____

_____   _____

Directions:

_____

_____

_____

_____

_____

_____

_____

_____

_____

_____

_____

_____

_____

_____

_____

_____

_____

_____

Recipe Name: _____   **Serves:** _____

Ingredients:

_____   _____

_____   _____

_____   _____

_____   _____

_____   _____

_____   _____

_____

Directions:

_____

_____

_____

_____

_____

_____

_____

_____

_____

_____

_____

_____

_____

_____

_____

_____

_____

_____

Recipe Name: _____ **Serves:** _____

Ingredients:

_____   _____

_____   _____

_____   _____

_____   _____

_____   _____

_____   _____

_____   _____

Directions:

_____

_____

_____

_____

_____

_____

_____

_____

_____

_____

_____

_____

_____

_____

A pickup truck tailgate makes a fine potluck
or picnic buffet table. Fill the back with a
galvanized tub of ice and soda, baskets of
plates, napkins and silverware and lots of
food...it's dinner, country style!

Recipe Name: _____ **Serves:** _____

Ingredients:

_____   _____
_____   _____
_____   _____
_____   _____
_____   _____
_____   _____
_____

Directions:

_____
_____
_____
_____
_____
_____
_____
_____
_____
_____
_____
_____
_____
_____
_____
_____
_____
_____
_____
_____

Recipe Name: _____ **Serves:** _____

Ingredients:

_____   _____

_____   _____

_____   _____

_____   _____

_____   _____

_____   _____

_____   _____

Directions:

_____

_____

_____

_____

_____

_____

_____

_____

_____

_____

_____

_____

_____

_____

_____

_____

_____

_____

My Favorite

RECIPES

NOTES

_____

_____

_____

_____

_____

_____

_____

_____

_____

_____

Recipe Name: _____ **Serves:** _____

Ingredients: .

_____   _____
_____   _____
_____   _____
_____   _____
_____   _____
_____   _____
_____   _____

Directions:

_____
_____
_____
_____
_____
_____
_____
_____
_____
_____
_____
_____
_____
_____
_____
_____
_____
_____
_____

Recipe Name: _____ **Serves:** _____

Ingredients:

_____   _____

_____   _____

_____   _____

_____   _____

_____   _____

_____   _____

_____   _____

Directions:

_____

_____

_____

_____

_____

_____

_____

_____

_____

_____

_____

_____

_____

Plan a recipe swap for your next block party or family reunion! Ask everyone to share the recipe for their dish, then slip the copies into sealable plastic bags for protection. Each family can go home with new favorites.

Recipe Name: _____   **Serves:** _____

Ingredients:

_____   _____

_____   _____

_____   _____

_____   _____

_____   _____

_____   _____

Directions:

_____

_____

_____

_____

_____

_____

_____

_____

_____

_____

_____

_____

_____

_____

_____

_____

_____

_____

Recipe Name: _____ **Serves:** _____

Ingredients:

_____ _____

_____ _____

_____ _____

_____ _____

_____ _____

_____ _____

_____ _____

Directions:

_____

_____

_____

_____

_____

_____

_____

_____

_____

_____

_____

_____

_____

_____

_____

_____

_____

_____

_____

_____

Recipe Name: _____   **Serves:** _____

Ingredients:

_____   _____

_____   _____

_____   _____

_____   _____

_____   _____

_____   _____

Directions:

_____

_____

_____

_____

_____

_____

_____

_____

_____

_____

_____

_____

_____

_____

On days when warmth is the most
important need of the human heart,
the kitchen is the place you can find it.
- E.B. White

Recipe Name: _____ **Serves:** _____

Ingredients:

_____   _____

_____   _____

_____   _____

_____   _____

_____   _____

_____   _____

_____

Directions:

_____

_____

_____

_____

_____

_____

_____

_____

_____

_____

_____

_____

_____

_____

_____

_____

_____

_____

Recipe Name: _____ **Serves:** _____

Ingredients:

_____   _____

_____   _____

_____   _____

_____   _____

_____   _____

_____   _____

_____   _____

Directions:

_____

_____

_____

_____

_____

_____

_____

_____

_____

_____

_____

_____

_____

_____

_____

_____

_____

_____

_____

Recipe Name: _____ **Serves:** _____

Ingredients:

_____   _____

_____   _____

_____   _____

_____   _____

_____   _____

_____   _____

_____

Directions:

_____

_____

_____

_____

_____

_____

_____

_____

_____

_____

_____

_____

_____

_____

_____

_____

_____

_____

_____

Recipe Name: _____ **Serves:** _____

Ingredients:

_____   _____

_____   _____

_____   _____

_____   _____

_____   _____

_____   _____

_____

Directions:

_____

_____

_____

_____

_____

_____

_____

_____

_____

_____

_____

_____

_____

_____

_____

_____

_____

_____

_____

_____

Recipe Name: _____   **Serves:** _____

Ingredients:

_____   _____
_____   _____
_____   _____
_____   _____
_____   _____
_____   _____
_____   _____

Directions:

_____
_____
_____
_____
_____
_____
_____
_____
_____
_____
_____
_____
_____
_____
_____

Visit a nearby farmers' market for fresh fruits & vegetables. You may also find baked goods, jams & jellies, pickles, craft items...all kinds of unexpected treats! With indoor markets, you can visit year 'round.

Recipe Name: _____ **Serves:** _____

Ingredients:

_____   _____

_____   _____

_____   _____

_____   _____

_____   _____

_____   _____

_____

Directions:

_____

_____

_____

_____

_____

_____

_____

_____

_____

_____

_____

_____

_____

_____

_____

_____

_____

_____

Recipe Name: _____ **Serves:** _____

Ingredients:

_____   _____

_____   _____

_____   _____

_____   _____

_____   _____

_____   _____

_____   _____

Directions:

_____

_____

_____

_____

_____

_____

_____

_____

_____

_____

_____

_____

_____

_____

_____

_____

_____

_____

Recipe Name: _____ **Serves:** _____

Ingredients:

_____   _____
_____   _____
_____   _____
_____   _____
_____   _____
_____   _____
_____   _____

Directions:

_____
_____
_____
_____
_____
_____
_____
_____
_____
_____
_____
_____
_____
_____
_____

Tuck jars of layered mixes in
an old-fashioned milk bottle
carrier...it's perfect!

Recipe Name: _____   **Serves:** _____

Ingredients:

_____   _____

_____   _____

_____   _____

_____   _____

_____   _____

_____   _____

_____

Directions:

_____

_____

_____

_____

_____

_____

_____

_____

_____

_____

_____

_____

_____

_____

_____

_____

_____

_____

Recipe Name: _____ **Serves:** _____

Ingredients:

_____   _____

_____   _____

_____   _____

_____   _____

_____   _____

_____   _____

_____

Directions:

_____

_____

_____

_____

_____

_____

_____

_____

_____

_____

_____

_____

_____

_____

_____

_____

_____

_____

Recipe Name: _____ **Serves:** _____

Ingredients:

_____   _____
_____   _____
_____   _____
_____   _____
_____   _____
_____   _____
_____

Directions:

_____
_____
_____
_____
_____
_____
_____
_____
_____
_____
_____
_____
_____
_____
_____
_____
_____
_____
_____

Recipe Name: _____ **Serves:** _____

Ingredients:

_____   _____

_____   _____

_____   _____

_____   _____

_____   _____

_____   _____

_____

Directions:

_____

_____

_____

_____

_____

_____

_____

_____

_____

_____

_____

_____

_____

_____

_____

_____

_____

_____

_____

Recipe Name: _____ **Serves:** _____

Ingredients:

_____   _____
_____   _____
_____   _____
_____   _____
_____   _____
_____   _____
_____   _____

Directions:

_____
_____
_____
_____
_____
_____
_____
_____
_____
_____
_____
_____
_____
_____
_____
_____

Old-fashioned canning jars make perfect
canisters for your country kitchen!

Recipe Name: _____ **Serves:** _____

Ingredients:

_____   _____
_____   _____
_____   _____
_____   _____
_____   _____
_____   _____
_____   _____

Directions:

_____
_____
_____
_____
_____
_____
_____
_____
_____
_____
_____
_____
_____
_____
_____
_____
_____
_____
_____

Recipe Name: _____ **Serves:** _____

Ingredients:

_____   _____

_____   _____

_____   _____

_____   _____

_____   _____

_____   _____

_____

Directions:

_____

_____

_____

_____

_____

_____

_____

_____

_____

_____

_____

_____

_____

_____

_____

_____

_____

_____

_____

Recipe Name: _____ **Serves:** _____

Ingredients:

_____   _____

_____   _____

_____   _____

_____   _____

_____   _____

_____   _____

Directions:

_____

_____

_____

_____

_____

_____

_____

_____

_____

_____

_____

_____

_____

Search out yard sales or auctions for vintage
tablecloths, dish towels, aprons and pillows with
colorful fruit motifs...they'll add instant nostalgia
to your kitchen.

My Favorite

RECIPES

NOTES

_____

_____

_____

_____

_____

_____

_____

_____

_____

Recipe Name: _____ **Serves:** _____

Ingredients:

_____   _____
_____   _____
_____   _____
_____   _____
_____   _____
_____   _____

Directions:

_____
_____
_____
_____
_____
_____
_____
_____
_____
_____
_____
_____
_____
_____
_____
_____
_____
_____

Recipe Name: _____ **Serves:** _____

Ingredients:

_____   _____
_____   _____
_____   _____
_____   _____
_____   _____
_____   _____
_____   _____

Directions:

_____
_____
_____
_____
_____
_____
_____
_____
_____
_____
_____
_____
_____
_____
_____
_____
_____
_____
_____

Recipe Name: _____   **Serves:** _____

Ingredients:

_____   _____

_____   _____

_____   _____

_____   _____

_____   _____

_____   _____

_____

Directions:

_____

_____

_____

_____

_____

_____

_____

_____

_____

_____

_____

_____

_____

_____

A weekend in the kitchen can give you rows and
rows of home-canned goodies! Invite friends over
to share your garden bounty by canning together.
The day goes so much faster when you can
laugh and chat together!

Recipe Name: _____   **Serves:** _____

Ingredients:

_____   _____

_____   _____

_____   _____

_____   _____

_____   _____

_____   _____

_____

Directions:

_____

_____

_____

_____

_____

_____

_____

_____

_____

_____

_____

_____

_____

_____

_____

_____

_____

_____

Recipe Name: _____ **Serves:** _____

Ingredients:

_____   _____

_____   _____

_____   _____

_____   _____

_____   _____

_____   _____

Directions:

_____

_____

_____

_____

_____

_____

_____

_____

_____

_____

_____

_____

_____

_____

_____

_____

_____

_____

Recipe Name: _____ **Serves:** _____

Ingredients:

_____   _____
_____   _____
_____   _____
_____   _____
_____   _____
_____   _____

Directions:

_____
_____
_____
_____
_____
_____
_____
_____
_____
_____
_____
_____
_____
_____
_____
_____
_____
_____
_____

Recipe Name: _____ **Serves:** _____

Ingredients:

_____   _____
_____   _____
_____   _____
_____   _____
_____   _____
_____   _____
_____   _____

Directions:

_____
_____
_____
_____
_____
_____
_____
_____
_____
_____
_____
_____
_____
_____
_____
_____
_____
_____

Recipe Name: _____ **Serves:** _____

Ingredients:

_____ _____
_____ _____
_____ _____
_____ _____
_____ _____
_____ _____

Directions:

_____
_____
_____
_____
_____
_____
_____
_____
_____
_____
_____
_____
_____
_____

Store fresh parsley in a glass
of water in the refrigerator to
make it last longer.

Recipe Name: _____ **Serves:** _____

Ingredients:

_____   _____
_____   _____
_____   _____
_____   _____
_____   _____
_____   _____

Directions:

_____
_____
_____
_____
_____
_____
_____
_____
_____
_____
_____
_____
_____
_____
_____
_____
_____
_____

Recipe Name: _____ **Serves:** _____

Ingredients:

_____ _____

_____ _____

_____ _____

_____ _____

_____ _____

_____ _____

_____

Directions:

_____

_____

_____

_____

_____

_____

_____

_____

_____

_____

_____

_____

_____

_____

_____

_____

_____

Recipe Name: _____   **Serves:** _____

Ingredients:

_____   _____
_____   _____
_____   _____
_____   _____
_____   _____
_____   _____
_____

Directions:

_____
_____
_____
_____
_____
_____
_____
_____
_____
_____
_____
_____
_____
_____
_____
_____
_____

Add 20 to 30% more flavor to your
cup of coffee...simply wet the paper filter
before brewing.

Recipe Name: _____ **Serves:** _____

Ingredients:

_____   _____

_____   _____

_____   _____

_____   _____

_____   _____

_____   _____

_____

Directions:

_____

_____

_____

_____

_____

_____

_____

_____

_____

_____

_____

_____

_____

_____

_____

_____

_____

Recipe Name: _____ **Serves:** _____

Ingredients:

_____   _____
_____   _____
_____   _____
_____   _____
_____   _____
_____   _____
_____

Directions:

_____
_____
_____
_____
_____
_____
_____
_____
_____
_____
_____
_____
_____
_____
_____
_____
_____
_____

Recipe Name: _____   **Serves:** _____

Ingredients:

_____   _____

_____   _____

_____   _____

_____   _____

_____   _____

_____   _____

_____

Directions:

_____

_____

_____

_____

_____

_____

_____

_____

_____

_____

_____

_____

_____

_____

_____

_____

_____

_____

Recipe Name: _____ **Serves:** _____

Ingredients:

_____   _____
_____   _____
_____   _____
_____   _____
_____   _____
_____   _____
_____

Directions:

_____
_____
_____
_____
_____
_____
_____
_____
_____
_____
_____
_____
_____
_____
_____
_____
_____
_____

Recipe Name: _____ **Serves:** _____

Ingredients:

_____   _____
_____   _____
_____   _____
_____   _____
_____   _____
_____   _____
_____

Directions:

_____
_____
_____
_____
_____
_____
_____
_____
_____
_____
_____
_____
_____
_____
_____

Make mayo go the extra mile! Flavor it with crushed garlic, chopped fresh herbs, lemon juice or even ready-made pesto.

Recipe Name: _____ **Serves:** _____

Ingredients:

_____	_____
_____	_____
_____	_____
_____	_____
_____	_____
_____	_____
_____	_____

Directions:

_____

_____

_____

_____

_____

_____

_____

_____

_____

_____

_____

_____

_____

_____

_____

_____

_____

_____

Recipe Name: _____ **Serves:** _____

Ingredients:

_____   _____
_____   _____
_____   _____
_____   _____
_____   _____
_____   _____
_____

Directions:

_____
_____
_____
_____
_____
_____
_____
_____
_____
_____
_____
_____
_____
_____
_____
_____
_____
_____

Recipe Name: _____   **Serves:** _____

Ingredients:

_____   _____

_____   _____

_____   _____

_____   _____

_____   _____

_____   _____

Directions:

_____

_____

_____

_____

_____

_____

_____

_____

_____

_____

_____

_____

_____

_____

_____

Potatoes, they grow small, and we dig them in
the fall and we eat 'em tops and all in Kansas.
- Kansas folk song

Recipe Name: _____ **Serves:** _____

Ingredients:

_____   _____

_____   _____

_____   _____

_____   _____

_____   _____

_____   _____

_____   _____

Directions:

_____

_____

_____

_____

_____

_____

_____

_____

_____

_____

_____

_____

_____

_____

_____

_____

_____

_____

_____

Recipe Name: _____ **Serves:** _____

Ingredients:

_____   _____

_____   _____

_____   _____

_____   _____

_____   _____

_____   _____

_____

Directions:

_____

_____

_____

_____

_____

_____

_____

_____

_____

_____

_____

_____

_____

_____

_____

_____

_____

_____

Recipe Name: _____ **Serves:** _____

Ingredients:

_____   _____
_____   _____
_____   _____
_____   _____
_____   _____
_____   _____

Directions:

_____
_____
_____
_____
_____
_____
_____
_____
_____
_____
_____
_____
_____
_____
_____
_____
_____
_____
_____

INDEX

Breakfasts

_____

_____

_____

_____

_____

_____

_____

_____

_____

_____

_____

_____

_____

_____

_____

_____

Appetizers

_____

_____

_____

_____

_____

_____

_____

_____

_____

_____

_____

_____

_____

_____

Soups & Breads

_____

_____

_____

_____

_____

_____

Index

INDEX

_____

_____

_____

_____

_____

_____

_____

_____

_____

_____

_____

_____

Main Dishes

_____

_____

_____

_____

Sides & Salads

_____

_____

_____

_____

_____

_____

_____

_____

_____

_____

_____

_____

_____

_____

_____

_____

_____

_____

_____

_____

_____

_____

Index

INDEX

Desserts

INDEX

Send us your favorite recipe!

and the memory that makes it special for you!* If we select your recipe for a brand-new **Gooseberry Patch** cookbook, your name will appear right along with it...and you'll receive a FREE copy of the book.

Share your recipe on our website at
www.gooseberrypatch.com

Or mail to:

Gooseberry Patch · Attn: Cookbook Dept.
2500 Farmers Dr., #110 · Columbus, OH 43235

*Don't forget to include your name, address, phone number and email address so we'll know how to reach you for your FREE book!

Since 1992, we've been publishing country cookbooks for every kitchen and for every meal of the day! Each has hundreds of budget-friendly recipes, using ingredients you already have on hand. Their lay-flat binding makes them easy to use and each is filled with hand-drawn artwork and plenty of personality.

Have a taste for more?

Call us toll-free at
1·800·854·6673

Find us here too!

Join our **Circle of Friends** and discover free recipes & crafts, plus giveaways & more! Visit our website or blog to join and be sure to follow us on Facebook & Twitter!

www.gooseberrypatch.com